Life in the
WOODS

MIKE ATNIP

ISBN: 978-1-941213-95-7

Cover photo: © shutterstock.com

All photographs in this book are by Mike and Daniel Atnip, with the following exceptions:

  Red fox, page 14-15: shutterstock.com

  Chipmunk, page 26-27: public domain

Printed in India

Published by:
TGS International
P.O. Box 355, Berlin, Ohio 44610 USA
Phone: 330-893-4828 | Fax: 330-893-2305 | www.tgsinternational.com

TGS001178

Do you want to take a walk in the woods? A sunbeam is lighting the path after a fresh shower of rain.

Bring your magnifying glass. Many of the creatures in the woods are small, like this snail. Look *down* at him as he putters across a leaf.

Bring binoculars too, since we will also want to look *up* at things like this cute gray squirrel.

Wait, come back! Don't be in such a hurry. God has many surprises for us if we go slowly and look around carefully.

See that caterpillar? He will someday turn into a moth or butterfly.

Okay, let's move on now, but slowly. One step, two steps, three steps, four steps . . .

Look! Another caterpillar, but this one is hairy. I wonder what kind of butterfly or moth it will become. God has many secrets in the woods.

Slowly raise your binoculars and watch that red-tailed hawk. He is watching something in the grass below him. Do you see those sharp claws?

Carefully turn now and look at
the gorgeous whitetail buck.
I think he sees us. Let's move
slowly so he does not run away.

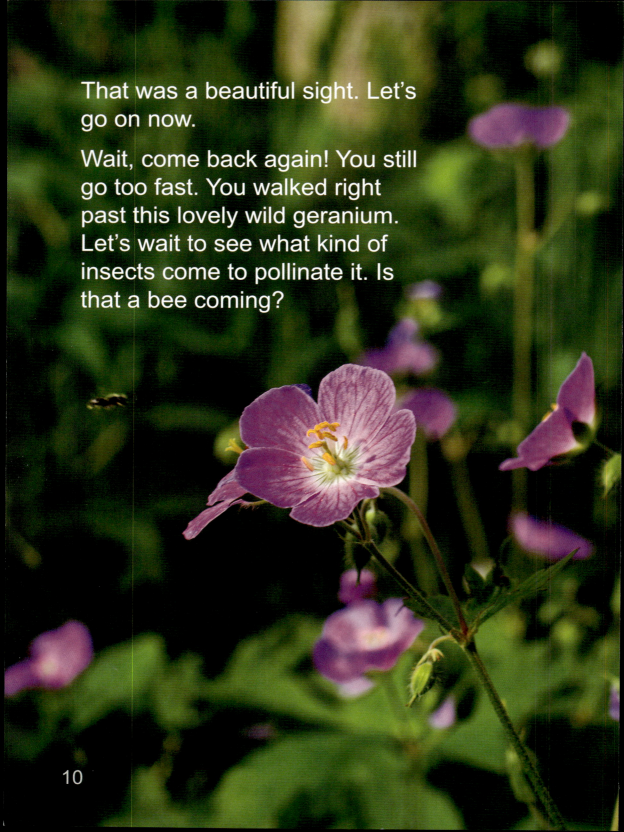

That was a beautiful sight. Let's go on now.

Wait, come back again! You still go too fast. You walked right past this lovely wild geranium. Let's wait to see what kind of insects come to pollinate it. Is that a bee coming?

I see something on that white flower. Oh, it's not a bee, even though it is the same color. It's a hoverfly. It's not fuzzy like a honeybee, and its wings are iridescent. That means they sometimes reflect the colors of a rainbow.

A snail has parked in the knothole of that tree. Is that his home, or is he using it as a hotel? Perhaps it's just a rest area as he travels up the tree.

Bend way over and look
through that thick bush.
A brown thrasher is
watching us from her nest.

It's not often that one gets to see a red fox, especially so close! His fur looks so cozy and soft. Do you wish you could touch it?

Carefully peek under those leaves and you will see a white moth. Let's slowly move around here and take a look at his face.

See that root over there?
Those are scarlet elfcups
poking out their heads.
Isn't it amazing how God
can make bright red pop
out of an old root?

17

Shhh! Look down there in the hollow with your binoculars.

Even though the wild turkey is far away, we must hold still. Turkeys have excellent eyesight and will run or fly away if they see movement. Is this turkey watching us? Notice all the colors on its feathers.

We do not need our magnifying glass to find this pheasant's back mushroom. It's large enough to sit on. Another name for it is saddle mushroom.

When this phantom crane fly wants to fly, it spreads its wings—and its legs—and lets the wind blow it away.

Ooooh! Isn't he cute! What if we had been looking up instead of down? We might have walked right past this whitetail fawn.

Aaah! I have never before seen a candy-striped leafhopper, and I have been in the woods many times. Yes, that is its real name. God made many wonderful things!

Ready to move on now?
Remember to go slowly
and look down as well as
up. No, that is not lettuce;
it's a green fungus.

God made fungi to break down wood so that it rots faster. This mushroom is actually the flower of a fungus that lives in the dead wood.

The chipmunk is enjoying a snack. What is he eating?

His tiny ears look like little flaps that could fold down. If we scare him, he will raise his tail and chatter as he scoots away at full speed.

Did you tell me to come back? You mean I'm the one going too fast now? I walked right past the green frog on the log! That round spot behind its eye is its ear.

This beetle's head sort of matches
my red hair. What unique colors!
God has so many surprises for us
in the woods.

I wonder what this slug is doing on the leaf. Let's watch him a little while and see what he's up to.

Now that is a charming set of flowers! Do you know what kind they are? I don't. Should we take some home for Mom?

Look, a crane fly! What beautiful wings! Although crane flies look like huge mosquitoes, they do not bite.

Pull out your
magnifying
glass again
and check
out his wings.
How pretty!

Sometimes it's fun to
find a high spot in the
woods and just enjoy
the floating clouds
and the many colors
God has given us.

Or just lie back on the leaves and look at the patterns of the tree branches as they reach for the heavens.

As we observe nature, our minds want to worship the Creator who made it all. It's good to have quiet time and meditate on Him.

Shhh! Step up here and let's watch this jumping spider try to catch the fly. See how he's crouched and ready to leap.

Oh, he missed!
Are you glad the fly
escaped? Or do you
feel sad that the spider
did not get his supper?

Check out the compound eye
on that fly. Hundreds of little
eyes make up one big eye.

That is not a dog; it's a coyote. Coyotes have bushy tails, long noses, and pointed ears. I wonder what he's staring at. Supper?

Do you like "chocolate" insects? The top one is a two-banded Japanese weevil. The bottom one is a *Piezogaster calcarator.* Now that is a mouthful! Since it has no common name, let's give it one. How about chocolate stink bug? Don't eat it, though!

Bull thistles have a lovely purple flower, but I hope they don't start growing in our pasture.

While roaming the woods, we may find large rocks like this one. Do you think you could climb it?

Oh, good, we get to see another spider before we go home. This looks like a garden spider. Notice how his colors—green, yellow, black, and white—match the plant he's hanging on.

Okay, time to head for the house. We saw many fascinating creatures in the woods. How did God think of creating so many colorful and unusual forms of life? Some of His creatures make us smile, and others just make us say, "Amazing!"

About the Author

Mike Atnip, his wife Ellen, and their son Daniel live in New Bedford, Ohio. Mike grew up among the cornfields of east-central Indiana, tromping through the fields and woods on a regular basis. Ellen grew up in southeast Pennsylvania, at the foot of Blue Mountain, but later lived in northern New York where the snow blows deep. Daniel was adopted from the tall Andes Mountains in Bolivia, South America, but has spent most of his life in the United States.

The Atnip family hopes that people young and old will see God's glory, power, and love in the creation of so many marvelous forms of life, and submit their hearts to Him as to a loving Father and Friend.

Mike welcomes reader response and can be contacted at atnips@gmail.com. You may also write to him in care of Christian Aid Ministries, P.O. Box 360, Berlin, Ohio 44610.

Christian Aid Ministries

Christian Aid Ministries was founded in 1981 as a nonprofit, tax-exempt 501(c)(3) organization. Its primary purpose is to provide a trustworthy and efficient channel for Amish, Mennonite, and other conservative Anabaptist groups and individuals to minister to physical and spiritual needs around the world. This is in response to the command ". . . do good unto all men, especially unto them who are of the household of faith" (Galatians 6:10).

Each year, CAM supporters provide approximately 15 million pounds of food, clothing, medicines, seeds, Bibles, Bible story books, and other Christian literature for needy people. Most of the aid goes to orphans and Christian families. Supporters' funds also help to clean up and rebuild for natural disaster victims, put up Gospel billboards in the U.S., support several church-planting efforts, operate two medical clinics, and provide resources for needy families to make their own living. CAM's main purposes for providing aid are to help and encourage God's people and bring the Gospel to a lost and dying world.

CAM has staff, warehouses, and distribution networks in Romania, Moldova, Ukraine, Haiti, Nicaragua, Liberia, and Israel. Aside from management, supervisory personnel, and bookkeeping operations, volunteers do most of the work at CAM locations. Each year, volunteers at our warehouses, field bases, Disaster Response Services projects, and other locations donate over 200,000 hours of work.

CAM's ultimate purpose is to glorify God and help enlarge His kingdom. ". . . whatsoever ye do, do all to the glory of God" (1 Corinthians 10:31).

Creation to Redemption

God created plants, birds, and fish in the first five days. On the sixth day, He created animals and man. At first man lived in harmony with God and the earth. But after Adam and Eve sinned, some people began to worship the creation rather than the Creator. Others began to selfishly destroy the creation in their pursuit of money, pleasure, or fame.

But God sent His Son Jesus into the world to rescue us from our sin. Jesus taught us to abandon the idolatry of nature worship and to be good stewards of God's creation. He died on the cross and rose again that we could be born again and enter the kingdom of God.

This kingdom of God is made up of those who have allowed Jesus to be King of their lives. Jesus leads these people into a harmonious relationship with God and teaches them to live holy, loving, and unselfish lives as they relate to people and things on this earth. They are in the world but not of the world and look forward to their final redemption in heaven.